# OWN WITH INTENTION

# ENDORSEMENTS

"It's about creating room for what actually matters!"

For me, as a business owner and mom of four, *Own with Intention* cut through the noise with wisdom that works in real life. Lauren's redefinition of minimalism gave me a fresh perspective. It isn't about having less stuff; it's about choosing intentional abundance. Your future self will thank you for reading this!

**SELAH HIRSCH**
CEO of Express My Brand,
author of *Pressing Pause: Finding Rest in a Restless World*

* * *

Minimalism isn't about owning less; it's about living more on purpose. It's a way of aligning your days with what matters most to you, so the life you're building actually reflects your deepest values. This book isn't just for people who want tidy closets; it's for anyone who wants to shape a legacy their children will feel in the way you love, lead, and show up.

In *Own with Intention*, Lauren Craddock invites us into a lifestyle shift that starts in the heart and spills into every corner of life. It's honest, hope-filled, and rooted in the belief that how we live today becomes the inheritance we leave tomorrow. If you've ever wondered how to live in a way your kids will be proud to remember, this is your blueprint.

**LINDSAY MCCARTHY**
Co-author of *The Miracle Morning for Parents and Families*,
co-founder of Fambundance

* * *

We were stuck as a family with too much to do and not enough time—at least, that's what I thought. It started with my being willing to trust Lauren and get rid of some excess stuff, which I did not do willingly at first. Then it turned into a way of life that has allowed us to do things we never imagined.

We now have three young boys, run multiple businesses, serve others, and impact millions as a family.

This could not have happened without the simple act of cutting down on the clutter and refocusing on what really matters.

Dream Big! Think Bigger!

**AARON CRADDOCK**

Entrepreneur, podcast host, husband of the author

# OWN WITH INTENTION

## 20 MINIMALIST PRACTICES TO CREATE SPACE FOR WHAT MATTERS MOST

LAUREN CRADDOCK

OWN WITH INTENTION

*20 Minimalist Practices to Create Space for What Matters Most*



Cover Design: Anton Khodakovsky
Interior Layout and Design: Brittany Becker
Editorial Team: Maggie Syrett, Ann Maynard, Rachel Maier

ISBNs:
E-book: 979-8-90372-003-3
Paperback: 979-8-90372-005-7
Hardcover: 979-8-90372-004-0

*Published by:*
Gordon Publishing
www.gordonpublishing.com

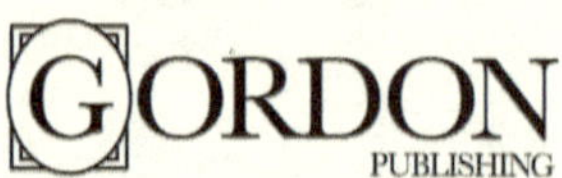

*To Aaron and my boys, for always supporting and cheering me on in my dreams. I love living this intentional life with you!*

Thank you for investing in this book.

I would love to stay connected with you beyond these pages. Scan the QR code below to connect with me and access additional resources!

Book Resources

# CONTENTS

# FOREWORD

**WE LIVE IN** a world full of noise, clutter, and distraction. In the midst of it all, it can be easy to lose sight of what really matters. That's why Lauren Craddock's message is so important.

*Own with Intention* is more than a book—it's an invitation to return to clarity.

Lauren's journey is one many of us can relate to. As a teacher, a mom of three young boys, and someone juggling the real pressures of modern life, she found herself overwhelmed, like so many of us do. But instead of numbing out or pushing through, she made a decision to live with more intention. To minimize. To realign. And it changed everything.

*Own with Intention* is an invitation for you to do the same. It's not about perfection or having a spotless home. It's not about getting rid of all your stuff. It's about making space for what really matters—freedom, clarity, purpose.

If you've ever felt stretched too thin or buried under the weight of "too much," this book will meet you right where you are. Lauren writes with honesty, wisdom, and warmth. Her story is relatable. Her practices are realistic. And her message is one we all need: you don't have to do it all; you just have to do what matters—on purpose.

I'm inspired by the action she took. And I believe this book will help you take meaningful action too, starting right where you are.

This book will help you take ownership of your time, space, and attention, so you can live with more purpose, presence, and peace.

Let it guide and challenge you. Let it lead you back to what matters most.

**JON GORDON**
18x best-selling author of *The Energy Bus* and *The One Truth*

# AUTHOR'S NOTE: HOW TO USE THIS BOOK

*Daring Readers,*

Welcome to the beginning of your minimalist journey! Before you return this copy to the shelf for fear of committing to yet *another thing* in your life, breathe. Breathe again. What I am about to share will give you more time, mental clarity, and purposeful pursuits. I will share practical tips that I've learned and experienced through my own journey. While I don't believe that minimalism is a "one-size-fits-all," I hope you will find some helpful advice in these pages. I hope you will see me as a friend. A friend sharing what has changed my perspective and my life. A friend who deeply cares that you also live intentionally and joyfully through the chaos and beauty of life. A friend who has extensively researched minimalism, because I felt that I was living to manage clutter rather than manage my purpose.

Minimizing is a personal process. Try to remain open to what works in your life. Remember, perfectionism isn't the goal; nor is it even attainable. The goal is to find freedom and physical relief from owning less. To have more time and energy to devote to other important tasks. To develop quick and simple daily tasks that keep your home clutter-free and ready for living! You will be ready for guests at a moment's notice, without worrying about cleaning up. You will pursue more dreams and create more of the life that you desire. You will save money. You will have greater peace of mind and will more easily recharge in your space. You will experience more joy and more freedom.

This journey is a lifelong one, like our fitness, meditation, and spirituality journeys. Sure, you can focus on minimizing for a time, but the transformative effects come from consistency and growth throughout your life. But even with the excitement and progress along the way, you will still have some clutter. You will have differences with loved ones about possessions; you will try and fail in your minimalism efforts; you will feel overwhelmed and exhausted at times. When these things happen, step back and refocus your perspective—remember why you decided to begin this journey. Then continue.

Minimalism is a catalyst that frees us to live, remember, and hope in what really matters.

Minimalism is worth it. It itself is neither the end goal nor the ultimate life hope. Minimalism is a catalyst that frees us to live, remember, and hope in what really matters. For me, that is faith, family, and purposeful living. Minimalism is a lifestyle that intentionally curates belongings, relationships, and other resources to create the most free and purposeful life possible. It is a process worth pursuing.

This book is built around twenty practices—simple, repeatable actions that have helped me shift from surviving clutter to living with clarity. They are best explored in order, because the perspective pivot must come before the lasting change. While it might be tempting to browse the chapters and jump to the practice you believe will be most beneficial, reaping the full transformational benefits first requires a mindset and perspective pivot before tackling the clutter. This will yield the greatest life change and happiness long term!

Are you ready to begin your journey and discover what minimalism can make room for in your life? I can't *wait* to see what you learn, what you release, and how your life expands. You don't have to do this perfectly. You just have to start.

Let's do this! Let's own with intention and make space for what matters most!

*Your friend,*

**LAUREN CRADDOCK**
Founder & CEO of *Own with Intention*
*www.ownwithintention.com*

## CHAPTER 1

# EXPLOSION: WHAT JUST HAPPENED?

**ONE AFTERNOON IN** February, I was frustrated and feeling significantly overwhelmed by stuff. I couldn't find my school badge, and my headphones were somewhere "safe." Our "drop zone" (counter and cabinets in the entry) had *exploded* over the past several weeks with bags, random objects, and piles of mail. I could barely open the junk drawer. Three massive baskets of unfolded clothes sat nearby. What had happened? Hadn't we minimized? Hadn't we done a good job of considering what we bought and brought into our home? We had worked diligently the last several years to change our perspective on stuff. So why was clutter overwhelming the physical spaces in our home and commandeering my mental and emotional energy? I felt the distress and despair of the chaos radiating from the piles of clutter.

Previously, I would have reprimanded my lack of discipline and proceeded to spend an hour decluttering. This time, instead of plowing through and cleaning up in frustration, I decided to take time to reflect. What had been going on in our lives over the past month or so? International travel. Sick babies. Husband out of town. No normal schedule or routine. All this left me with little mental or emotional bandwidth beyond my daily spiritual habits, teaching, family time, and working out. I was *worn out* and could barely muster the energy to deal with the mounting mess. Day after day, the chaos overwhelmed me and continued to multiply, reflecting my internal state.

This time, instead of berating myself for not being more disciplined, I gave myself grace and carved out time to rest and find personal peace through prayer, journaling, Scripture reading, and walking in nature. Only then did I tackle the drop zone. An hour later, the clutter was conquered, extras were discarded, and our possessions were returned to their rightful places. More importantly, though, I had a sense of calm and inner peace knowing that I had taken care of myself and my self-esteem through this process—a beautiful reminder that I am more important than stuff and that I can intentionally choose self-care. The accumulation of clutter had brought about the disintegration of habits and of my state of mind. This moment taught me to pause, reflect on my state of being, and then make small, purposeful changes.

This moment taught me to pause, reflect on my state of being, and then make small, purposeful changes.

The following chapters document the stories, challenges, successes, failures, and practices of my minimalism journey. They are based on my personal experience; your path will no doubt look different. You may use some or all of these practices; you may even create some of your own to help you achieve the life you want. Minimalism is not a one-and-done decluttering process. It is a *lifestyle* in which you dictate what enters and exits your home, based on the needs and desires of your life. Above all, I hope this book serves as an inspiration and reminder to you that you are more important than stuff.

Now, let's go back in time and see where my journey began.

## CHAPTER 2

# ONCE UPON A TIME: BEFORE THE PIVOT

•○—•○•—○•

MY HUSBAND, AARON, and I met at the University of Alabama during my first week of college. He was a junior, and I was a freshman. We quickly became best friends and began dating a couple of years later. We dated for eight months before getting engaged and then married five months later. We were young, in love, and optimistic about our future. Aaron was working a government job in the transportation bureau, making around $28,000 a year. I wasn't earning, because I was finishing school.

Our first rental was a two-bedroom duplex with a carpeted kitchen (yes, carpeted!) and bugs in the walls—for $450 a month. We were given almost all the furniture in our home, apart from a red loveseat that we bought at Goodwill. We didn't have much. Nor did we have the means to buy more, so we kept whatever was given to us. We rarely turned down freebies in case we needed them later. We were extremely resourceful in repurposing and repainting things to make the duplex our home. We even found a large freestanding cabinet on the side of the road that we spray-painted black and used as a pantry in our kitchen.

I marvel at our beginnings as a couple! I'm beyond grateful for the blessings and the lessons we learned. We quickly understood the value of a dollar and how hard work and strategic planning could help us achieve our dreams.

We saved and scraped and ate a lot of rice and beans. After our first year, we both obtained decent-paying jobs—me as a teacher, and Aaron as a digital manager in the trucking industry. Aaron also started a side-hustle selling coins. We were beginning to feel more financially sound. We moved to a larger rental with tile in the kitchen (woohoo!) and a backyard for our two five-pound dogs, Cooper and Cammi. We continued our frugal lifestyle and found options through scholarships to both work full-time and get our masters' degrees.

"We quickly understood the value of a dollar and how hard work and strategic planning could help us achieve our dreams."

It was a crazy time of our lives, but we embraced the struggle and built endurance and grit, knowing that we were setting ourselves up for a more stable future for our family. We hunted for bargains from flea markets and estate sales, because we now had the means to begin purchasing some of our own furniture and decorations. Our first large purchase was a deep freezer that we placed in the guest bedroom! I was all about freezer cooking and was beginning to lean into my desire for systems and learning how to maximize efforts.

After six years of marriage and two rental properties, we bought our first home: a beautiful, two-story farmhouse-style home in Tuscaloosa, Alabama. Suddenly, we had almost double the space of our previous rental; we justified the space by explaining that we were preparing for future kiddos. It was our first dream house, with amazing closet space, something I knew to be a big deal from all the house-buying shows. I added labeled baskets to the closets, designating closets for specific purposes. We even had a three-car garage, in which we were able to park both cars, house our deep freezer, and store our garage stuff.

All this space seemed to be such a blessing, and my organizing and systematizing skills were hard at work. At this point, we had figured out our design style and purchased all our own furniture. We kept most of the little things that had been given to us, because I wanted to be prepared for every possible scenario.

A couple of years passed, and I noticed that areas were beginning to feel disorganized and cluttered. We had acquired my husband's grandmother's Coca Cola collection, stored it in the third bay of the garage, and had great plans for selling individual pieces, along with other odds and ends that Aaron acquired with the intention of flipping. We installed a five-basket-high shelving unit in the laundry room to store weeks of dirty laundry. I bought about twenty gray baskets and set about organizing and labeling the pantry, just like I had recently seen on an organizational show. We built shelves in the top of our garage to hold our holiday decorations and bins of childhood toys—just in case we needed them for our future kids.

"I noticed that areas were beginning to feel disorganized and cluttered."

I bought items in bulk, because it "saved" money. Some bulk purchases included five toilet cleaning solutions, fifty rolls of toilet paper (maybe a good problem in 2020!), four big bottles of dish soap, a thousand napkins, several backup items for all our personal products, three shelves of candles and holders, pounds and pounds of almonds and walnuts, and so on. I justified that we had the closet space and I was *great* about being prepared with backups for all we would need. Between my husband's collector tendencies and my prepping practices, everything began to spill out from its designated spot. Believing that containing the items was the real issue, I bought more bins and more labels.

The constant need to gather scattered items and reorganize them into bins was exhausting and disheartening, to say the least. This was definitely *not* how I wanted to spend my time. It was around 2018 that my social media searches led me to information about decluttering. I became obsessed, believing that decluttering was the ultimate solution I had been searching for. I read *everything* I could find on the subject. My first step, documented on social media, was to go through my clothes and pare them down by about half. I loved the idea of developing a capsule wardrobe to simplify my morning routine. I naively thought that a massive one-time effort was the key to forever keeping the clutter at bay.

Until it wasn't the ultimate saving system I thought it would be . . . Stuff continued to pour into our home through gifts or Amazon purchases, some promising to make our lives easier or better. I continued pressing forward, consuming and organizing more content, looking for the perfect system somewhere out there. I loved Marie Kondo's work and began decluttering things that no longer served me or brought me joy.[1] I devoured texts about habits: *Tiny Habits*,[2] *Atomic Habits*,[3] and *The Power of Habit*.[4] I found I was developing and solidifying personal habits of working out and reading, so I attempted to create cleaning habits too. I read dozens of cleaning plans and constructed my own plans to make my home "always presentable." I hypothesized that if I applied my newly researched methods and worked even harder, I would achieve lasting progress and beautifully organized closets. With a lot of time and effort, my home did become a little more tame, yet I felt like I was constantly holding back a sea of chaos. And those just-in-case-I-might-need-them items were still lurking in the shadows.

I later came to understand that this scarcity mentality, the fear of not having enough and of not having what I needed in the future, was confining me to a life of clutter. This mindset had been developed in my childhood, growing up in a middle-class family. We valued hard work and earning our way in life. As I worked through high school and college and earned scholarships, this mentality of grasping and hanging onto things deepened.

Of course, this scarcity mentality had been my survival mantra in the early years of our marriage, helping us make the most of what we had. We were so grateful for everything we received from generous friends and family. We didn't want to appear ungrateful or wasteful. Yet I was starting to recognize that maybe, just maybe, I didn't have to cling to every single thing out of fear that it would prove useful someday. Maybe I could learn to let some things go and live with a different mindset. Maybe my perspective could pivot. This inkling began forming on the edges of my mind.

> "The fear of not having enough and of not having what I needed in the future was confining me to a life of clutter."

Our life drastically changed over the next two years. My husband started his own company. COVID hit and shut down the entire world. My first son was born. My husband became sober. I began teaching at a university while still teaching elementary school. Amid these massive life changes, we were still desperately looking for a way to live more simply. We wanted to better enjoy the beauty of life as working parents. We wanted more time, more calm, and more purposeful lives. We were tired of the hamster wheel of cleaning, tidying, organizing, and managing clutter.

Then it happened! We stumbled upon Joshua Becker's books *The More of Less*[5] and *The Minimalist Home.*[6] Our lives were completely changed, not overnight, but they were revolutionized in a way that we could never go back! I finally realized why all my organization and decluttering techniques hadn't worked. I didn't need more initiative, more discipline, more bins, or new folding techniques. I needed a *perspective* pivot of my stuff, time, and other resources. It felt like my blinders were removed, and I was finally aware of my belief that more was better. More Christmas lights would make me happier; more Pyrex bowls would help me meal prep; more decorations would beautify my home; more books and pictures would make me feel more at home; more backup products would ensure that we never ran out; more beauty products would aid my search for that perfect item for my skin and hair; more clothes would provide variety and freedom of style; more subscriptions would deliver an array of entertainment choices; more coffee mugs would allow me to pick my mood for that day; more rotations of toys would keep my son entertained; more, more, and more.

I had completely bought into consumerism, believing that goods would bring me happiness and a better life. And I paid for it dearly with my time, energy, space, relationships, and finances.

I walked away from reading the books, feeling like there was a glimmer of hope for a simpler life that didn't involve hours of cleaning and tidying every evening. I realized that I was caught in the cycle and addiction of consumerism, with no consideration of whether the items were actually needed or how they affected my time and space. Our stuff was taking up more than just closet space. It was stealing time, consuming mental energy, and creating a never-ending to-do list. I was shocked at how much of my time and energy didn't match up with what I most valued in life. I was determined to reclaim my life by becoming minimalist.

Joshua Becker's books were my entry point to considering the minimalist lifestyle. Previously when I'd heard the term, I had assumed that these people just ate rice and beans (been there, done that), owned one fork and one plate per person, and had nothing on their walls. While this might be true for some, minimalism doesn't provide a list of rules, regulations, and code of ownership that dictates whether you qualify as a minimalist. Reflecting on Becker's texts and internalizing what resonated with me, I was able to create my own understanding of minimalism in *my life* and begin making my way forward.

I define minimalism as the lifestyle of assessing and curating resources, time, activities, and relationships to create the life you most desire. It's the initial and ongoing process of asking yourself if something (item, relationship, process, etc.) is needed, how much is needed, and whether it delights your heart. Minimalism involves getting rid of things that are no longer useful and savoring what you *intentionally choose* to keep in your life; it is choosing one thing instead of other things, deliberately crafting your life and stuff. In a sense, we are all minimizing something: possessions, time, money, energy, potential. I finally chose to purposely select items and resources in my life to maximize my potential, energy, joy, and impact. I was done serving and managing clutter; I wanted to manage my consciously designed life and purposes.

"I finally chose to purposely select items and resources in my life to maximize my potential, energy, joy, and impact. I was done serving and managing clutter; I wanted to manage my consciously designed life and purposes."

My husband and I began systematically sifting through our rooms, asking ourselves what we used and liked in each room. It was amazing the amount of articles we were holding onto that we never used: pie pans, fondue pot (it had sat, unused, in a cabinet since we were married), books I would never read again, shirts from high school, my college graduation gown, several pairs of old tennis shoes for yard work that I never did, weirdly shaped vases, mismatched bed sheets, dry-rotted golf clubs, and much more.

Soon after we began this minimizing process, we felt strongly in our spirits that we no longer belonged in Tuscaloosa. This took us by surprise, because we were planning on living there forever. But as people of faith, we leaned into discussion and prayer to determine what a change would look like. After much research, we decided to spend a week in Austin, Texas—top of our list—to see if it was indeed the city for us. During that week, I had several interviews and landed a teaching job, we found an awesome house to rent, and we enrolled our son in a nearby daycare. We returned to Tuscaloosa and soon found out we were pregnant with our second son. We also received a cash offer to rent our home for the year! Truly, our minimizing process couldn't have come at a better time, as we donated and trashed tens of thousands of items. Two months later, we loaded up our cars and two large U-Haul trucks and began our caravan out west to Texas.

We experienced the most amazing peace, excitement, and clarity when we started our minimalism journey. Do I think we would have heard our God's prompting and moved to Austin if we hadn't been diligent in beginning our minimizing process? Probably. I do, however, believe that the action of minimizing made us completely open to new opportunities. And this, in turn, made us open to the possibility of moving across the country and beginning a new life.

We settled into our rental in Austin and still had a lot of unused items—an entire garage bay full of stuff: extra sets of china, at least fifteen flower vases, gameboards we no longer played but might someday play with our kids, and so on. Aaron began buying old books for a dollar each from the library bookstore to sell—well, this was his collector and entrepreneurial intention! For months, we had boxes of books lining the hallways. Just when we had discarded thousands of items, additional objects were creeping in to fill the space. I knew this had to change, especially with another baby on the way. We challenged our perspective to pivot even more, as we began refining several minimalist practices that enabled us to reap huge dividends of time and space.

Let's discuss how to successfully minimize before we continue with my story.

## CHAPTER 3

# WHERE TO BEGIN: PERSPECTIVE PIVOT

THIS CHAPTER IS probably the most important part of the minimizing process, which is why I like to begin here. Unless your perspective about stuff changes, you can declutter all you want, but possessions and the lure of consumerism will continue to gobble your time and energy. I know this from personal experience. Consumerism is addictive, and, like most addictions, the mind and soul must heal and gain proper perspective before the behaviors will change.

I live in an American culture that daily advertises new clothes, technology, travel experiences, apps, movies, beauty products, and . . . the list is endless. The entire culture is based around consumerism and the idea that more stuff will make us happier, beautiful, successful, popular, and purposeful in life. But this idea could not be further from the truth! I shared how the clutter of this consumerist lifestyle eventually overwhelmed our home, demanding so much of our time and energy to clean, organize, and find items.

Upon reaching this point of disillusionment, I asked myself what I considered—or should consider—as most important in my life. My answer: pursuing intentional *relationships* with family and friends, finding *peace* with myself, deepening *faith* in God, caring for my *health*, living with a fulfilling *purpose* of making the world a better place, and bringing others hope through *education*. I envisioned what the environment of this fulfilling life would look like. I imagined high-quality, beautiful yet simple places that allowed for gatherings of friends and family; an inspiring place overlooking nature to write and think; spaces that contributed to and supported my life's vision—no clutter. I recognized that so many of the items in my life were irrelevant to the full, intentional life I was longing for. At the end of the day, I wanted people to remember me for the love and intentionality I showed in my relationships and work rather than the number of books, clothes, dishes, homes, and items that I collected.

> "Our entire culture is based around consumerism and the idea that more stuff will make us happier, beautiful, successful, popular, and purposeful in life. But this idea could not be further from the truth!"

I also witnessed both sets of our parents going through *their* parents' belongings once they had moved or passed away. It was such an undertaking, and honestly, many things were given away. Personally, I want my kiddos to be left with resources that they can use or easily give to those in need. I don't want them sorting through shelves of dozens of vases and candles, wondering why in the world their mom "needed" them. What legacy do I want to leave for my family?

Through all these realizations, I recognized the need for a statement, or mantra, that I could use to remind me of the perspective pivot I had experienced. A pivot remains grounded but can shift direction.

This is precisely what I had done. Through experiences and reflection, I had clarified my life's purposes and desires and put down deep roots in those ideas. I then pivoted my mindset to embrace a different way of approaching stuff. The statement that emerged as I walked through the process was: "I am minimizing to have a simpler, joyful, purpose-filled life focused on faith, family, and impact." If an item doesn't align with my statement, then I gratefully release it, knowing that, in its place, I will receive more physical space as well as mental lightness.

I encourage you to draft your own statement as you begin working through your perspective pivot regarding possessions. This will ground you in your purpose for minimalism, especially when you get stuck sorting through some particular items.

"I am minimizing to have a simpler, joyful, purpose-filled life focused on faith, family, and impact."

First, take some time to reflect on what your core priorities are. They should be central to your being as a person and specific to you. These are the aspects of your life that you deem non-negotiable to you and your purpose. It is essential to clarify priorities before minimizing, because they will majorly contribute to your "why" for reducing clutter. I invite you to work through the following to help you consider your core priorities and craft your statement.

- Who is most important in my life?
- What character traits do I value and most try to embody?
- What is my purpose here on earth? What impact do I hope to have on others around me?
- What does it feel like to intentionally walk in my purpose?
- Now, looking at your responses, condense them into a handful of words to ground you in who you are and what you are about. What are those words?

Once you've identified your core priorities, spend some time reflecting on the process of minimizing. Use the following questions to help you gather a deeper understanding of why you are committing to this journey.

- Why am I minimizing?
- What positives come from minimizing?
- What does a life with less stuff look like for me?
- What barriers do I anticipate during this process?

Now, looking at your responses, sum up your minimizing "why" in a few words.

You may like to write your own perspective statement reminding you of your perspective pivot. Alternatively, you can use some of the handful of words from the reflection responses you just jotted down to complete the template sentence that follows. Write down your statement, so you can reference it as you begin to sort through items in your home. It will help you remain focused on your vision and the life that you want to create.

*"I am minimizing in order to (words from minimizing responses):"*

________________________________________

________________________________________

*"I am focused on (your core priorities):"*

________________________________________

________________________________________

## CHAPTER 4

# MINIMALIST METHODS TO APPROACH THE MADNESS

•○—•○•—○•

**BEFORE WE JUMP** into the minimalist process that I use, I need to remind you that minimalism looks different for everyone. Every person sets their own thresholds for quantity of stuff. Over time, your thresholds may change. Minimalism is not a one-time decluttering effort; it is not a style or trend; it is a *lifestyle* of consistently and consciously evaluating your resources to determine if they are helping you thrive or distracting you from your purpose. Minimalism involves intentionality in both adding and giving away possessions. James Clear writes in *Atomic Habits*, "You don't have to be the victim of your environment. You can also be the architect of it."[7] You can create the life you want through intentional choices, habits, and hard work. I can affirm that minimalism works and is worth it.

There is a plethora of information about how to minimize and declutter possessions. In my experience, minimalism falls into one of three methodical categories: Total Home Reset, Zone-Focused Reset, and Daily Reset. All three of these methods can help you restore order in your home by methodically dealing with clutter in your home. I have used all three methods; certain times of life lend themselves to a specific method. Whatever method you use, the goal is always to propel you forward to cut the clutter and create the life you want. While I highly recommend that you eventually go through everything you own, it can happen gradually over time. Remember, you are the architect of your life.

## Method 1: Total Home Reset

> "Minimalism falls into one of three methodical categories: Total Home Reset, Zone-Focused Reset, and Daily Reset."

I highly recommend that everyone beginning a minimalist lifestyle plans a Total Home Reset with their family at some point. This may not be the starting point for you in this season, but I truly believe that the full benefits of minimalism come from addressing *all* possessions in your life, not just the junk drawer or the cluttered closet. The Total Home Reset involves going from room to room and category by category through all your items. This may take a solid weekend or several months. Either way, develop a plan with your family with clear starting and ending points.

Before we look at specific suggestions for tackling this method, let me remind you how I define minimalism. It is the lifestyle of assessing and curating resources to create the life you most desire. It involves parting with things that are no longer useful and savoring what you intentionally choose to keep. That is what you will be doing by using this method: assessing the usefulness of your possessions in view of your life's vision and intentionally keeping items that support that vision. Remember: own with intention! Here are some suggestions for success.

- Keep your perspective statement clearly posted to constantly remind yourself of your "why" for minimalism. At some point, it will get more difficult, so reminding yourself of your why is imperative.
- Clearly post clarifying questions (more on this in The Process chapter).
- Set aside time to tackle the minimizing process. Daily dedicated time keeps the momentum going; larger chunks of time allow for greater progress in a shorter window of time. At the time of each of our Total Home Resets, we moved into a new home. This accelerated the process and gave us a deadline for minimizing. Depending on the number of possessions you have, and on your schedule, you may be able to set aside a full week to address all your possessions. Or you may just have fifteen to thirty minutes every evening. Don't let time hold you back. Get started, even if it's just five minutes a day.
- Gather all necessary supplies: trash bag, giveaway box (that can also be donated), perspective statement and clarifying questions, people, bins, baskets, and Post-it notes or label maker. Post-it notes allow you to clearly and temporarily label a space, bin, basket, or shelf as you return items to their designated locations. I prefer to completely minimize a given area and label with Post-it notes before I decide on more permanent labels needed for the area.
- Follow The Process, outlined in the next chapter.

## Method 2: Zone-Focused Reset

The Zone-Focused Reset addresses minimizing specific areas in your home. I most often notice that I need this method when a particular area is exploding with clutter and disorganization.

My husband and I had been on the minimalist journey for about a year and a half. We tracked giving away 34,055 items during this time. I had completed two Total Home Resets during our move to Texas and our subsequent move across the neighborhood. I was reaping the benefits of more time due to less cleaning, more calm due to less clutter, and more clarity due to our confidence in ridding our lives of items that didn't support our vision. I felt great about our minimalist journey . . . until I couldn't find my school badge . . . and then I couldn't locate my AirPods. I was frustrated that I couldn't quickly locate necessary items despite all the progress we had made. Chaos had overtaken our drop zone. I had recognized the growing stacks of clutter and overflowing drawers but quickly brushed it all aside due to more pressing matters. Stacks of mail, kiddos' coloring pages from school, jackets, shoes galore, random contents of my purse dumped out, remnants of Valentine's Day gifts from students, my badge (somewhere), my AirPods (also somewhere), water bottles, and trash from my car. This used to be a once-a-week or more occurrence that would require hours of cleanup time. Now, thanks to minimalism, I find it happens about once a month at most, just not normally to this extreme.

Sometimes Zone-Focused Resets come from times of exhaustion and clutter explosions. Other times, you can simply identify one area that you want to minimize to help your life become more efficient and effective. I recently began my classroom minimalist journey by targeting my top desk drawer where I store my most used items: pens, markers, stapler, highlighters, stickers, Post-it notes, and so on.

Here are some steps I use to target various areas of my home and restore order:

- Decide on a clearly designated space to minimize: a drawer, shelf, closet, cabinet, or desktop. Be specific and targeted in your identification—focusing on an entire room is not specific enough. Target a smaller area to clearly define its importance and purpose in your life.

- Decide on the use of the space. When you decide how you want to use the area, you will have a better idea of which items belong and which need to go.
- Minimize the space (see The Process chapter).
- Guard the space. Once you minimize the space, do *not* let items into the space that should not be there. By practicing guarding the space, you are developing the discipline to say no to what does not belong and intentionally put away the items that do. Over time, this can build momentum, endurance, and clarity in your minimalist journey.

## Method 3: Daily Reset

Total Home Resets and Zone-Focused Resets are life-changing, but they are not long-lasting. The Daily Reset is the systematization of habits in your life that continue your journey of the minimalist lifestyle.

“Our lives are full of mini habits. By nature, we strive to make patterns with our actions.”

I love to read and learn about habit formation, because our lives are full of mini habits. By nature, we strive to make patterns with our actions. As James Clear states, “You do not rise to the level of your goals. You fall to the level of your systems.”[8] The Daily Reset helps us continually monitor the items arriving in our home and give them a specific place (closet, trash can, recycle, etc.) rather than saving them in a stack to deal with later. Clutter compounds, so the sooner you can deal with incoming items, the better!

Remember the drop zone explosion? The following day upon arriving home, I felt peace and accomplishment when I walked in the door. I decided to set a ten-minute timer on my watch to put away the incoming items right then to prevent a future explosion. To my surprise, it took slightly less time than that to put away three lunch boxes and their containers, a bag of bottles, a school bag, trash from the car, papers from school, and mail from the mailbox. I even got my oldest kid to help with putting away shoes and socks and washing hands. By the end of ten minutes, we were unpacked and ready to play. What a relief! This Daily Reset of immediate unpacking works well for my family. Does that mean it always happens? No, but my husband and I work hard to deal with today's stuff before today is over. This majorly restores order in our home.

Here are some of my Daily Resets:

- Nightly resetting the kitchen—loading the dishwasher, wiping counters, putting leftovers in the fridge
- Making the bed as soon as I get up in the morning
- Putting laundry away on the day it's completed
- Resetting the living room (aka having my kids put away their toys every evening)
- Putting away all items from school and work as soon as we get home
- Dealing with each day's incoming mail

You may be wondering how these are minimizing habits. They certainly just sound like daily cleaning or resetting the room habits. I included these, because they are essential to maintaining minimalism in my home. Dr. John Maxwell often states that "consistency compounds."[9] I rephrase it when discussing minimalism: clutter compounds! A small pile tends to attract more items, creating a much larger pile of clutter (think toys, mail, laundry, dishes). Dealing with small amounts of items along the way and maintaining simple yet effective systems keep your mind and space clear, freeing you up to better live your life's purpose.

## CHAPTER 5

# THE PROCESS

**I HAVE SPENT YEARS** researching and refining the process I use to approach possessions in our home. This book is the culmination and systemization of the practices and methods that have worked in my life. The Process outlined in this chapter is the simple and repeatable process that I use in all three of my methods. I encourage you to first try The Process before attempting to adapt it. Each step is essential, keeping you grounded in your perspective pivot while also gaining momentum in minimizing. This is The Process.

### 1. Intention: Set an Intention for the Area

Decide what you want the area to be used for. Will it be a plastic container cabinet? A daily recharge area with your journal, books, and pens? A cleaning supply cabinet? Knowing what you want the space to be used for is essential, because it helps you clarify what belongs and what should be removed. This space's intention can change over time, so don't spend precious time debating the question. This particularly applies to areas like the kitchen. Sometimes it takes time and living in an area to decide whether the space is best used for your original intention. So I encourage you to make a quick decision about the space's intention so that you can start the minimizing process.

## 2. Empty: Empty the Space One Item at a Time

This is essential. Previously, I found that I became completely overwhelmed any time I emptied everything into the room to declutter or organize. More often than not, I ended up with cluttered piles sitting out for a while. Instead, empty one item at a time, asking yourself clarifying questions as you go. In this way, you can stop at any moment and have a manageable pile to deal with. This approach lives much better than pulling all the clutter out at once.

## 3. Question: Ask Three Clarifying Questions

### *#1. While you empty one item at a time, ask yourself, "Do I use this item?"*

If your answer is *yes* or *sometimes*, set the item aside. You will return to this item at the end of emptying the space. I encourage you to group like items as you go. For example, if I am emptying my junk drawer, I group together the pens that I will use, the gift cards I will use, and the scissors I will use rather than simply dumping all the "use items" into one pile. Organizing a dumped pile requires additional organization. Work smarter, not harder!

If your answer to the use of an item is *no* or *rarely*, put it in the trash or give it away. You should have designated bags and boxes labeled "trash" and "give away" to put your items directly into. I advise against making visual piles of trash and give away. Remove these items from sight by putting them in a bag or box. Make sure you are comfortable with giving away the bags and boxes—it doesn't make sense to stuff a bag you want to keep with giveaways. Recycle your cardboard boxes or grocery bags. Again, just clearly label the bags and boxes.

### *#2. Analyze the "Keep Items" by asking, "Do I like this item?"*

This is a quick practice for everything you plan on returning to the newly minimized and intended area. It's important for us to like the items we use. I want feelings of calm, joy, and peace when I use items in my home, not frustration and disgust. If you don't like it, don't keep it! If it is the only item in a necessary category, make a note of this in your phone and keep it for now. Set a goal for yourself to purchase an item that could replace this item—something that you would use *and* like. Once you have the replacement, exchange the item rather than keeping both. For example, I had a manual can opener. I was exceedingly frustrated every time I tried to use it, but it was the only way to open cans in our home. I eventually purchased an electric can opener (love it!) and got rid of the manual can opener. This shows a smart, intentional purchase that served a purpose in my life and brought greater peace.

### *#3. "How many of this item do I need?"*

I have found that the first two questions (Do I use it? and Do I like it?) are the most essential questions when minimizing an area. The next analysis impacts long-term minimalism. As you prepare to return items to an area (or as you consider the items in an area), ask yourself how many of the same item you need for one specific purpose. In my most recent Total Home Reset, I discovered I owned four pie pans. I think I have only made one pie in my entire life! My family did not need this many pans. I happily gave three away (my husband insisted on keeping one; #compromise). The imposed limit of one pie pan helped me select the one I wanted to keep and allowed me to joyfully release the others to people who would actually use them. Some items (like the pie pans) may only require that I keep one. Others (like hair ties) may be dictated by the size of the allotted space (see Practice 6).

Don't get stuck on this third question. Make a quick, logical decision and move on. In all my years of minimizing, I've only discarded two items that I needed later: a stapler and a mini sewing kit. Honestly, those were easy replacements, and the freed space was worth it in the meantime.

## 4. Return: Does the Item Match the Space's Intention?

Once the space is empty, put the "use items" back one at a time, asking yourself, "Does this item fit the intention of this area?" If the answer is yes, return the item to the area in an organized state, grouping together by like item and using baskets and bins if you already have them. If the item does not belong, set it aside to be moved somewhere else. If you immediately know where the item should go, you could take it to the designated area, as long as you don't get sidetracked by other areas in need of minimizing!

## 5. Transfer: Move Other Items to Where They Belong

Once you have returned all "use items" to their organized area, take the remaining items that don't fit the area's intention to the part of your home where you think they belong. If you are not sure, choose the best location based on the current use. For example, I found Band-Aids and cough drops in my purse. As I didn't need them there, I moved them to the medicine box in our main bathroom. If you are unsure of where the item should go, make a quick decision, knowing that the worst-case scenario is that you'll eventually have to find a new location for the item.

Know that you may also get frustrated that you are returning an item to an area that has not yet been minimized and organized. Take a deep breath . . . and put it there anyway. You will eventually reach this zone, but the item needs a sensible, logical home, and it cannot return to the newly minimized area.

## 6. Celebrate!

If you are anything like me, I forget, or don't celebrate, my progress on personal goals. Take a moment to admire your hard work. Progress, not perfection! Snap a picture and share it with a friend or family member. Do a happy dance! Oprah Winfrey so perfectly reminds us that "the more you praise and celebrate your life, the more there is in life to celebrate."[10] Celebration cultivates positivity, creating momentum in your life. Be proud of your efforts and success. Your actions just helped you get closer to your desired life. Review your perspective statement to remind yourself of your why. And celebrate your progress!

## 7. Be a Guardian!

Picture in your mind what a guardian looks like. Maybe you envision Gandalf blocking the path saying, "You shall not pass!" Maybe you imagine Jedi with lightsabers or fully armored knights. Now envision yourself as this guardian. As cheesy as this may sound, envisioning and fully feeling yourself as the guardian is important. You are becoming the guardian for your desired life. You are intentionally standing firm against mindless consumerism and deciding what is allowed in your life and home. You are the guardian for more peace, time, energy, and money in your life. You don't have to be a victim to clutter, things, or situations. You have the power within you to *choose* your lifestyle—and the things in it. If you need to print out a picture of this guardian to remind yourself of your power and your role for intentional living, do it!

Take your guardian role seriously. Do not, I repeat, do not let items into your newly minimized area if they don't belong. This is where the Gandalf image resonates with me, and I tell the item, "You shall not pass!" You worked hard to clear that space; now, guard it with intention and find another place to put the item. Sometimes items sneak through. When this happens and you notice them, immediately remove them and deal with them accordingly—trash, giveaway, or transfer.

> "You are the guardian for more peace, time, energy, and money in your life. You don't have to be a victim to clutter, things, or situations."

## 8. Don't Stress

Don't stress if you don't know whether to get rid of an item. When indecision happens, reread your perspective statement, envision the goals of your minimized life, and then ask yourself your clarifying questions. If you're still undecided, keep the item for now. You can either put it in a box with a designated departure date if it hasn't been used by then or simply organize the item back into your home. If you choose the latter, please make sure that it is in a *visible* location. It can still be in a closet, but make sure you can see it. This is extremely important, because whenever you see the item, you will remember to use it. I found that, over time, some items became less necessary or meaningful to me than before, allowing me to finally let them go.

Here is a simplified list of the steps we have discussed. Write them on an index card to help keep you on track in the minimizing process:

1. Set an intention
2. Empty
3. Question: Do I use it? Do I like it? How many do I need?
4. Return
5. Transfer
6. Celebrate
7. Guard
8. Don't stress

## CHAPTER 6

# LET THE LIFESTYLE BEGIN: GIVE YOURSELF GRACE

•o—•O•—o•

**AT THIS POINT,** you are armed with everything you need to successfully begin your minimalist journey. You have spent time pivoting and reshaping your perspective and have learned The Process that I use to live a successful minimalist lifestyle. You are ready to begin implementing it in your own life. The twenty practices that follow are helpful ways that motivate me when I feel stuck, gamify my progress, and address specific problem areas when minimizing. I use the term *practice*, because it implies consistent actions that yield results. Strategies are simply plans; practices mean I am taking action. I hope they will do that in your life too.

You may decide to use some of these practices and find that they are not all necessary for you. Remember, you already have the simple, repeatable process to be successful in cutting clutter and creating your desired life. I have used all these practices at some point in my journey and hope they will continue to propel you forward.

I want to pause and give a final reminder to all type A people who have systematized a calendar schedule for the process, gathered boxes galore, and recruited a team of family members ready to minimize the house. Remember: you are human. Give yourself grace in this process. Progress, not perfection. You will thrive at times and fail at other times. The minimalist lifestyle requires patience with yourself as you confront years of habits and consumerist perspectives and seek to pivot to a different way forward in your life.

Remember my drop zone explosion from the beginning of the book? I considered what I wanted it to be used for and the habits I would need to implement, or tweak, to use this space effectively to benefit and support our lives. I wanted it to be a place to store daily items: backpacks, bags, purses, keys, and incoming mail. I knew that maintaining it would require a daily purging of what came into our house. I started timing how long it took me to open the mail and either put it in the trash or in a pile for my husband to address. It took less than three minutes! What! The mental load of "going through the mail" was exaggerated in my head. Taking ten minutes upon arriving home to deal with the mail, put shoes away, empty bottles and lunchboxes, and hang up jackets kept the space sane and set us up for success in approaching the rest of the evening. Simultaneously, I began teaching my oldest son to put away his items and help empty his lunchbox. Parents should not have to bear the load of the household alone; kiddos can help support the systems in the home, even from a young age.

Strategies are simply plans; practices mean I am taking action.

My reason for sharing this story is to highlight my biggest takeaway: I am human. This explosive incident was a pivotal point for me as a minimalist, a mom, and a human. The clutter simply spotlighted my exhaustion and internal human state. I was not less of a person; in fact, it was a helpful reminder that I am a finite being on earth, with limited capacity, energy, and emotion. I do not say this as an excuse but as a reminder that I can extend grace to myself, learn, grow, and act differently in the future.

## PRACTICE 1:

# TRACK ITEMS

•○—•◯•—○•

**LET'S RETURN TO** our rental in Austin, Texas, when our garage bay overflowed with items, books lined the hallway, and another baby was soon to make his appearance. We felt stuck in our minimalist journey and knew that another layer needed to be shed. Clutter was compounding, so we used one of my favorite practices to attack the problem: track items.

My husband and I both thrive in challenges, tracking systems, and games. I thought gamifying the minimalism journey might help us. I stuck a Post-it note on the wall to begin tracking how many items we gave away or threw out. Although we had given away tens of thousands of items before moving to Texas, I was ready to narrow down our items even more. It became addictive; throughout the day I found myself hunting for at least one item I could get rid of. It seemed like a celebration every time we put a number on the wall. And every number represented the ways we were intentionally saying yes to time, freedom, space, and necessary or beloved items. We systematically worked through closets, kitchen cabinets, and so on, putting our hands on every item to determine whether to keep it or add it to our list. In this second Total Home Reset we identified items that we no longer needed after moving. The more we minimized, the more confident we became in what we wanted to keep and what we could release.

Fast forward one year. We had eliminated about 34,055 items from our home, not including daily trash or mail. I couldn't believe that we had that many items to begin with, much less that we had that many items to discard during a second Total Home Reset! And amazingly, I still felt that we had more items than we needed. In that season, tracking helped us reach a deeper level of minimalism to get closer to the freer life and better stewardship of resources that we envisioned.

"We had eliminated about 34,055 items from our home, not including daily trash or mail."

## PRACTICE 2

# THE BOX-UP BOOST

•○—•◯•—○•

**OUR ITEMS BEGAN** clicking into the thousands at a furious pace as our second son's birth rapidly approached. A few months out, a house came on the market in our neighborhood that we loved. It was the perfect size for our growing family, and it backed up to beautiful Texas hill country. Our offer was accepted.

Moving is a great way to literally put your hands on every item. In *The Minimalists* documentary on Netflix, Joshua and Ryan describe the practice of boxing up everything in the house, only unpacking what was needed over a pre-decided time period, and donating boxes of items that hadn't been used by the allotted time. Living with unopened boxes sounds like a lot of stress to me, so I would have never done this. However, our moving process replicated their practice and helped me deal quickly with our full garage and closets.

We moved across the neighborhood while I was on maternity leave. I was so encouraged that we only needed one large U-Haul truck. That means we had eliminated an entire truck load of stuff while living in our Austin rental for seven months. Once again, we touched every item, eliminating even more items that we did not need and some pieces of furniture that did not fit our new house. Previously, we would have stored the furniture in the garage—just in case. But 99 percent of the time, the furniture never left the garage until we moved to the next location. Styles change every five to ten years, anyway, so there was no sense in continuing to save furniture in case I might use it later. It was an incredible blessing to give and sell furniture to others that needed it. How much better use of a resource!

At this point, we began experiencing a great return on investment with our time and mental space. It took us about 50 percent less time in the evening to put away toys and dishes. We also felt lighter in energy. The massive decrease in clutter helped my mind feel freer and more creative, because I was not continuously visually bombarded with items that needed to be put away. My point: clutter is an energy sucker.

**PRACTICE 3**

# INVENTORY ITEMS

**AS WE PUT** away items in our new home, we began looking at the number of items we had in each category. For example, we had enough bath towels for the four of us to use four bath towels a week. We had developed the habit of doing laundry once a week, so there was no way we needed to store sixteen bath towels. We decided to keep two a week per person plus two extras. Taking an inventory and quantifying the items allowed us to clearly see that we still didn't need everything we had.

> "Taking an inventory and quantifying the items allowed us to clearly see that we still didn't need everything we had."

We decided on quantities for kitchen towels and rags, baby bibs, cans of beans, entertaining glasses, water bottles (I am majorly guilty of amassing water bottles), kids' cars, kids' pants, pens, shoes, work pants, pairs of pajamas, sunglasses, and so on. I found that I didn't need five pairs of sunglasses, fifty pens, twelve water bottles, or enough pajamas to wear two pairs per day for a week! I decided how many of each item to keep and chose my absolute favorites in each category.

It was a relief that I no longer had to store the extras, nor look through large piles of items to find my favorites. Gone was the guilt every time I looked in my drawer and almost always passed over an item in favor of my favorites. Another bonus was that I had a clear space for each item and could find them when I needed them.

We were so proud of our minimizing progress, finding such freedom in owning less. It was amazing to park two cars in our two-car garage! Items had specific places in our house. Life continued to progress as the boys grew and I settled into my new teaching job. My husband's business was thriving; our relationships with others were growing through a couple different groups. We found that we now had more time and energy to invest in our work, family, and others.

PRACTICE 4

# ORGANIZE WITH EASE

MULTIPLE BOOKS, TV shows, podcasts, and social media platforms are dedicated to the organization of homes. I love seeing pictures of organized spaces and learning how people piece together their possessions. Even before we learned about minimalism, I was obsessed with organization. I truly believed that if I found the right type of baskets and ordered everything by type, we would never have the chaos of clutter. Boy was I wrong! For organization to be effective, minimalism must happen first and then continue. Dumping all your clutter into organized baskets still means that you have the same amount of stuff—it's just stored away from view! In this case, your attitude to stuff hasn't changed. Your shopping and acquiring habits haven't changed. Your giving patterns haven't changed. This is one firm reason that I believe minimalism works, because it requires people to evaluate and pivot their perspective.

I would like to share some tried and tested organizational ideas that I developed over years of obsessive reading about habits and organization. But they will only work if you have minimized first.

## 1. Everything Should Have a Place

When everything has a specific place, it is easier to keep things tidy. Furthermore, putting an item back in its designated spot immediately after using it allows you to easily find it next time.

When everything has a specific place, it is easier to keep things tidy.

## 2. Organization With or Without Baskets, That Is the Question

I love using plastic bins and baskets in most situations. I use varying sizes of gray plastic bins in my pantry. They help me group common items and bring order to the various sizes and colors of items. I always make sure that my baskets are easily visible and accessible. I choose baskets that are easy to see inside. Some people choose to use clear bins for household supplies and toys for better visibility. Make sure your bin allows for easy access, so that items don't remain hidden and forever forgotten. In other scenarios, you may not want to use bins, because you want to clearly see everything you have. I do this with clothes, because I'm committed to wearing everything I own. The only clothes I put in baskets are either out of season or maternity.

So, ask yourself if your baskets are helpfully grouping items together or hiding them. If it's the latter, you may be hiding items so successfully that you're hanging on to items you no longer need or like!

## 3. Label, Label, Label

Label your bins with a label maker or permanent markers. I love my label maker—it's small and easy to use and allows me to efficiently change labels when needed. Labels help me return items to their designated locations and remind me what is in a basket or bin.

## 4. Keep the Line of Sight Clutter-Free

Keep surfaces and open spaces clear. Too many decorations, utensils, or appliances cause a cluttered line of sight. Only display the most necessary or loved items. Taking ten seconds to put my bathroom lotions away in a cabinet instead of displaying them on the counter provides me more peace and calm in my space. Experiment by removing an item off a counter or off a wall for a while to see how you feel. Most of the time you will probably feel relieved and not add it back.

## 5. If It Doesn't Fit the Flow, Find a New Space

If you aren't sure where an item should be stored, try a space and see how you live with it. For example, I found that I used my candle lighter way more when it was in our drop zone drawer than when it was in a household bin. It was not out in the open creating visual clutter, but removing the one step of opening a bin allowed me to more easily use the lighter. I want to be able to use all my stuff. Another example is when I moved dishes and pots and pans in the kitchen to better fit the flow of cooking and storage. Give yourself permission to try a system or space and then change it if you need to. Find the best flow for the time of life you are in now.

PRACTICE 5

# START SIMPLE, FINISH STRONG

MOMENTUM IS JUST as important as perspective when minimizing. Even after years of my minimalist journey, I still hit roadblocks and have zero motivation. Starting somewhere small and manageable is the best way to begin when you feel stuck—your brain recognizes the progress and the win. As you begin to string together more and more small wins, it is habit-forming and addicting. In *Tiny Habits*, Fogg reminds us: "We're not aiming for perfection here, only consistency. Keeping the habit alive means keeping it rooted in your routine no matter how tiny it is."[11] Our goal is to make minimalism a transformative catalyst in our lives through tiny actions.

"Our goal is to make minimalism a transformative catalyst in our lives through tiny actions."

Please do not begin minimizing your most sentimental items, like photos, keepsakes, baby clothes, and souvenirs. It would be the equivalent of me trying to run an ultramarathon without any training. Not only do I not have the stamina and endurance, but I would struggle mentally and emotionally along the way. Honestly, I would probably never make it to the finish line. If by some miracle I did, I would be battered in all senses of the word, and so disheartened that I would never attempt a long race again. I don't want that to happen with you and minimalism. Curating what is in your life is an endurance race built on strength and endurance through tiny, repetitive actions.

Here are some simple areas to help develop your minimizing muscles before you tackle more complex projects:

- Your purse or backpack
- Your kitchen counter
- Your junk drawer
- Your water cups and water bottles
- Your laundry room cabinets
- Your kitchen sink cabinet
- Your pet's space
- Your nightstand
- Your pantry

These places are small enough that they can easily be minimized in one sitting. And you probably won't encounter anything incredibly sentimental in these areas. Use The Process to help you gain momentum and strength for this journey.

## PRACTICE 6

# BOUNDARIES, NOT BULK

•○—•◯•—○•

**DO YOU WANT** your home to become a warehouse or a life-giving refuge? Toilet paper, paper towels, kid snacks, books, kids' clothes, shoes, games, my clothes—these are just a few categories that have quickly multiplied in my home over the years when left unchecked. Early on in our marriage, I was a big fan of buying everything in bulk. I thought stockpiling was the best option for preparedness; I now believe the complete opposite. There may be situations and families that benefit from buying large quantities of an item. A young couple with zero children in a three-bedroom rental, however, did not need to buy and *store* in bulk. At that time in our lives, I truly had enough meat in the freezer, boxes of toothpaste, paper towels, toilet paper rolls, and cleaning supplies from a local wholesale store to support us for six months or more.

While this is necessary if you are going off the grid for that length of time, I would now highly discourage my younger self from making these choices. The problem was that I filled any empty space we had with duplicates and back-ups. I then needed to organize and rearrange those items for months (or sometimes years: yes, I had several bottles of toilet cleaner that lived in three of my houses). Filling empty spaces creates more clutter to maintain while you are hopefully using these items. This eats up energy, time, and space.

Through minimalism, I have learned that it is essential to quantify the amount of space you are willing to dedicate to any single item. For example, I dedicate one large shelf of our bathroom closet to paper towels and toilet paper. Only when we take the final ones from the shelf to the kitchen or bathroom do I order another package online. Even with a family of five, this happens only every couple of months. Simplifying the process and setting boundaries means I am not storing items in bulk all around my house. Another example is that I have a single bin for my sons' snacks. I don't purchase more until we have worked our way completely to the bottom of the bin. I also limit myself to one dresser drawer dedicated to workout apparel and won't exceed this drawer even though I am a huge fan of leggings!

"The problem was that I filled any empty space we had with duplicates and back-ups."

You get the picture. Trust me, space and your mental calm are way more valuable than 99 percent of the items that you store in your house. Consequently, set your boundaries for how much space you allow for items, and stick to them. This practice eliminates waste, provides accountability for incoming items (see next chapter on Mindful Exchange), saves money, and keeps you on track for maintaining a minimalist lifestyle. Boundaries create freedom, even in a closet.

## PRACTICE 7

# THE MINDFUL EXCHANGE

SOMETIMES ITEMS NEED to be replaced due to wear and tear. If this happens, make an exchange for the item and employ a one in, one out action. For every item that you bring into your home, another item should leave. This doesn't mean that you buy another outfit and get rid of a kitchen dish. While the kitchen dish may also need to go, it is best to use this mindful exchange practice in similar categories. This holds you accountable in keeping your preset amounts in check and various categories in their contained spaces.

My two-year-old son recently received several books and a stuffed animal for his birthday. This was a great opportunity for me to look at his book collection and determine the least-favorite, least-read, and most-damaged books. We mindfully analyzed the stuffed animals. We selected one for each incoming item and disposed of them. This helped us guard the minimized space and curate the items, so that only the favorite and most-used items were kept.

My five-year-old son is now old enough to comprehend our conversations about possessions and about giving to others. He has learned that an exchange happens when an item enters the home, and we involve him in choosing which item needs to be given or thrown away. This gives him agency as well as teaching him to exercise his muscles of choice and minimalism. Mindful of our consumerist culture, we want to instill different values and perspectives in our sons, with the hope that they will learn to identify their own consumerist thresholds over time and intentionally own items.

The Mindful Exchange does not work the other way: one item out and one in. So it does not mean that because you removed three shirts, you can now buy three new ones. At this rate, you will never reach your desired minimalist threshold or make impactful progress in your minimalist efforts. Instead, use the Mindful Exchange when items need to be replaced due to damage or when you receive gifts.

## PRACTICE 8

# FINISH BEFORE REFILL

**I LOVE DISCOVERING NEW** products. More accurately, new products easily discover me through the help of social media and people. Over the years, I've come to recognize my susceptibility to hoping that the latest beauty products and gadgets will be the perfect life-changers that I've been waiting for my whole life! I long to continuously improve myself, which means that I am eager to try new products to "fix" whatever aging, acne-prone, chippy nails, or frizzy hair issues I have at any given moment.

Before I began my minimalist journey, I was willing to spend money to find the holy grail of any category I "needed." While I discovered some products that I still use today, most were quickly replaced with "better" options or disappointedly stuffed to the back of a drawer, because they didn't live up to my expectations. I collected hundreds of beauty products, from face wash to nails to makeup to hair treatments. My one bathroom cabinet overflowed into three large drawers. I reached a point where the clutter was overwhelming, and I couldn't get ready in the morning without struggling to find products, digging through piles of items, and feeling anxious.

When we discovered minimalism, I decided this was a major area where I needed to pivot my perspective. I was looking to the latest trends to fulfill me and to fix my beauty ailments. While I don't think that beauty products are inherently bad, I do think my perspective on them was damaging. I was looking to them to bring a version of perfection and was disappointed time and time again. So while I wanted products that were safe and worked well, I didn't want to be caught up in hype about the newest products; nor did I want to look to them for fulfillment. I was exhausted with the physical clutter as well as the mental overload; my search for perfection was emptying and soul-draining. Rather, my hope was that they would take care of my body, provide longevity and health, and support my looks and life—not take over my life.

While I knew I needed to get the clutter under control with my initial purging, I was more concerned about keeping it clutter-free for the future. I worked on pivoting my perspective: beauty products should care for my body rather than define me. I also began thinking longer before buying beauty supplies. Despite my best efforts, I found clutter and some of my old buying habits creeping back in, causing more chaos.

After minimizing a couple more times, I finally realized that I needed to *finish* products before replacing them. This has honestly been one of the most difficult practices for me to implement, but it has majorly helped me keep clutter out of my bathroom. Soon after I decided on this practice, I saw an ad on social media offering a new clean hair regimen that would make my hair smooth. My first reaction was to try it. I then remembered my promise to myself to finish before refilling. I decided to wait until I had used up my current shampoo and conditioner. This would keep me from storing half-finished bottles of shampoo and conditioner in my cabinet but would allow me to try the new regimen—eventually.

Already, I know some of you may be thinking, "What if the new shampoo works better for my hair than the current one? I'll miss out on having smooth hair for the next month!" If you live with a fear-of-missing-out mentality, you will most definitely accumulate stuff. The fear of missing out on the newest styles, cars, beauty lines, diets, and social media platforms will leave you constantly consuming, addicted to clutter and possessions. I can tell you, from my own experience, that it is exhausting and not fulfilling. At the end of the day, having the latest and greatest clothes will not matter.

I want to set my life on a meaningful path, focused on good and peaceful things. I have discovered that being present with my family, self, friends, and students and expressing gratitude for today's simple joys and blessings helps me pivot my mind from the fear of missing out.

“The fear of missing out on the newest styles, cars, beauty lines, diets, and social media platforms will leave you constantly consuming, addicted to clutter and possessions.”

## PRACTICE 9

# ROUTINE REFINEMENT

**I KNEW THAT I** wanted to simplify my morning and evening routines to gain back time. I was tired of spending so much time getting ready and wanted to instead spend more time living and making memories. I decided it was time to refine my routines! I began narrowing down my beauty products to those that I used the most. If a product was only occasionally used and not super transformative in my health, wellness, or care, then I used it up and decided not to replace it.

Based on my revelations in the previous chapter, you can imagine that I am a sucker for free beauty products. However, I figured that most of the time, a company is giving away free products to try and add another product to our routines. For me, free products rarely proved to be transformational or effective. Most times, when I tried a free product, I would just end up with more products taking up space in my cabinets.

I learned to identify my go-to daily products. Fewer products equaled less storage and less time getting ready in the morning. One example is that I did not see much difference using makeup primer, so I decided to let the free sample go and focus on clean skin and quality foundation. Another example is that I rarely used my deep conditioner bottle and did not notice a change in my hair's frizziness. So I let it go and stuck with my daily shampoo and conditioner.

What routines in your life might need refining? Here are some suggestions to get you started.

1. Identify areas of your life in which you would like to save time. Getting ready? Ordering groceries? Cooking dinner? Meal prep? Prepping for your workday? Winding down from your workday? Which routines could use a refinement in effectiveness and efficacy?
2. Ask yourself the following questions:
    a. Is it a location issue? Do you need to move products or items to a new location to streamline the habit? Do you need to group items in a common location?
    b. Is it a clutter issue? Do you have too many items in the space where the habit occurs?
    c. Is there something you are incorporating into the routine that is not needed? Try to do without it for a while and see if it helps simplify the routine.

## PRACTICE 10

# PASS IT FORWARD

A COUPLE YEARS AFTER we started our minimalism journey, the clutter threshold was beginning to feel overwhelming again, so I launched into my third Total Home Reset. I was tracking pretty well, but I hit several bumps where I struggled with my clarifying questions. Part of the struggle was that my life had changed considerably, as I now had a young baby and a toddler, I had started a new job, and I was more deeply plugging into our community and church. My time allocation was different, and honestly, I had not taken the time to revisit my perspective statement on why I had committed to a life of minimalism. Consequently, the shift of time—but more importantly, my perspective pivot away from my "why"—had caused crowded spaces and an accumulation of items.

Pressing pause on my Total Home Reset, I decided to take some moments to recenter my perspective. I took two steps for inspiration: I read my perspective statement to remind myself of my goals, and I looked to another minimalist, Joshua Becker. I was particularly struck by what he shared about giving to specific organizations.[12] Previously, we had only given to the trash can or to a local thrift store. While there is nothing wrong with either of these, I resolved to check out some other options in our greater Austin area.

A Google search led me to two local organizations concerned with refugee relocation and homelessness. I read through the types of donations they each received and considered the families that we could impact for free. I stepped into our kitchen and surveyed some areas I had been struggling with. Sudden clarity, joy, and excitement rose up in me as I imagined refugee families using my items to make delicious and healthy meals as they began their lives anew.

I realized that my minimalist efforts could go beyond my life, my joy, and my home; they could touch the lives of others who needed resources and items that I could provide.

I realized that my minimalist efforts could go beyond my life, my joy, and my home; they could touch the lives of others who needed resources and items that I could provide. I then began thinking about how amazing it would be for my five-year-old to accompany me and see the people behind our minimizing. Giving can seem so abstract until you see, meet, or imagine the people who are directly impacted by your donations. Not only did this practice help me get unstuck but it highlighted the joy of passing items forward to those who would benefit from them.

## PRACTICE 11

# COUNT THE INFLOW

•○—•◯•—○•

**I BEGAN THINKING ABOUT** the number of items entering my home. We had spent a couple of years tracking what we released from our home, but did we know how many items were coming through our door each week? I began an experiment to track incoming items and familiarize myself with the full picture. I counted every grocery item, every piece of mail, every package and its contents, artwork from the boys' preschool, gifts, and so on. I clocked in at 233 items across a seven-day period. This was lower than I had been bracing for, but we had been minimizing for a while. I dread to think how much would have entered our home before that. We had collected 233 items even with *mindful* purchasing of only what we needed.

I counted again several months later and calculated a crazy 695 items entering in a week! Why such a discrepancy? The first inflow count was a normal purchasing week. The second represented a week where many of our reorders hit at once. I did not despair over this; the practice had simply helped raise my awareness.

Why would I take time to count incoming items across a week? *Awareness.* I was intentionally seeing *every* incoming item, which helped me identify trends. I wasn't trying to adjust my purchasing habits during those two weeks; I was simply looking for data to illuminate where I spent my money. *Accountability.* Did I impulse buy? Did I scroll online, clicking on alluring items? Did I impose any limitations or discipline on purchases, like waiting a certain amount of time before buying something I "needed"? How did I define *need* and *want*, and should they be reevaluated?

I wouldn't make this a weekly practice for the rest of your life. It's more like going to the doctor once a year for a checkup. Think of counting the inflow as a necessary but occasional checkup to raise awareness and provide accountability. You can then consider the questions I posed in the preceding paragraph and begin adjusting your buying habits.

Your goal is for most of your incoming items to be quickly disposable, like food. Some items might slowly disappear over time, like medicines and toilet paper. Keep tabs on these items, since they are coming to take up residence with you for a while. Determine how many you need and how much space you can allot to these items. Another goal would be that very few items entering should stay permanently; these items may include clothing, toys, books, bags, tools, and home decor. The more of these items that enter your home, the more stuff you have to deal with long-term. Ideally, you would employ the Mindful Exchange with most of these more permanent items to prevent unmanageable accumulation.

## PRACTICE 12

# TIME IT TO TAME IT

HAVE YOU EVER found yourself dreading daily household tasks because of the amount of time they take? Do you envision hours of cleaning, cooking, and picking up? For me, my perceived estimate of how long tasks took was not accurate. To develop a more realistic sense of time, I looked to my timer.

I had already found it to be a useful tool with my writing and schoolwork. By designating a block of time to work on a specific task, I was more engaged and focused, knowing there was a clear finish line. Whenever I would begin to wander or work on other tasks, I could quickly redirect myself to the current assignment, knowing there was a designated time limit.

Success with the timer in these areas of life encouraged me to use it in addressing minimalism and tasks around the house. I set the stopwatch function to time how long tasks actually took me—tasks like emptying the dishwasher, folding laundry, picking up toys, unpacking lunch boxes and bags after school, and vacuuming the downstairs. I was feeling resistance to these tasks at this stage of my life and needed a jump start.

First, I set blocks of time (ten or twenty minutes) to tackle several tasks at a time. While this helped, I was still dreading certain tasks. I determined to conquer the problem by gathering data to counteract my resistance. So I began timing myself in these everyday tasks. I was astounded. Do you know what I found? Most of the dreaded tasks took considerably less time than I had built up in my mind. They also took way less mental and emotional energy when I handled tasks as they arose versus waiting until things built up, such as multiple baskets of laundry. Remember, clutter compounds! It's better to handle less clutter or a small task immediately than wait until there's more. More requires more time, more energy, and more space.

## Time Taken to Complete Household Tasks

| DREADED TASKS | TIME TO COMPLETE |
|---|---|
| *Emptying dishwasher* | *4 minutes* |
| *Folding one load of laundry (ugh, least favorite chore)* | *8 minutes* |
| *Nightly routine: unpacking lunch boxes, cleaning up dinner dishes, unpacking backpacks, laying out clothes for tomorrow* | *20 minutes* |
| *Vacuuming our first level* | *9 minutes* |
| *Wiping down toilets and sinks in three bathrooms* | *5 minutes* |

Once I knew the true amount of time these tasks took, they seemed less daunting. Instead of being overwhelmed by the prospect of a quick wipe-down and vacuuming for the week, I knew it would only take about fifteen minutes. Wow. Fifteen minutes for a cleaner space for the week. Totally worth it. The purpose of this practice was to break down my resistance to daily habits that could either eliminate or compound that day's clutter. Having a more realistic sense of time better prepared me to act as the guardian, tackle the day's responsibilities, and restore order in my home.

I also developed the one-minute timer tactic. After my third son was born, I seemed to be in a consistent state of frenzy at home. I know hormones, lack of sleep, and a recovering body contributed greatly to this, but I was starting twenty tasks and never finishing them until right before bed. My mind felt like it had twenty tabs of unfinished projects open at all times; I was swamped with mental fatigue and compounding clutter. It was time to use the timer to tame the chaos.

> "Most of the dreaded tasks took considerably less time than I had built up in my mind."

B. J. Fogg points out that "in order to design successful habits and change your behaviors, you should do three things. Stop judging yourself. Take your aspirations and break them down into tiny behaviors. Embrace mistakes as discoveries and use them to move forward."[13] I took his advice and used the timer to break tasks down into the smallest perceivable increment of time. I knew I could convince my brain to do anything for one minute, and that I could hit pause on everything else for a minute. I was eager to try out this new practice.

The effect was remarkable. I could accomplish a surprising amount of tasks in one-minute segments throughout the day. I could make my bed, put away ten items of clothing, change out the laundry, open five pieces of mail, pick up twenty toys, and empty a quarter of the dishwasher. It was just the momentum catalyst I needed to begin taming those open tabs in my mind. It elevated my mood and allowed me to be more present with my kids outside of the one-minute increments.

This practice of using the timer to tame chaos is linked to the Daily Reset routines and habits in your life. Clutter compounds without Daily Reset. In that season of my life, I needed inspiration, momentum, and very small increments of time to help me accomplish these daily habits. Time It to Tame It provided all three.

## PRACTICE 13

# PRESERVE THE PRECIOUS

SOME PEOPLE NEVER get started on their minimalist journey for fear of getting rid of sentimental items. May I be the first to tell you: don't let this stop you. Going through sentimental items isn't as difficult as imagined if you minimize everything else first.

We know that when we exercise regularly, our muscles get stronger, and we develop endurance. A similar phenomenon happens through the minimizing process. The more you minimize, the better you become at deciding between items. You gain a better sense of what you need and want to keep. Therefore, I recommend waiting until you have minimized most of your other possessions before working on sentimental and precious items such as pictures, heirlooms, and souvenirs. By this point, you will have gained a clearer sense of what is important to you and will have a stronger muscle for minimalism.

The process is the same as for any other item. Continue to remind yourself of your perspective statement. Remember to be gracious to yourself. It is a process.

In my childhood, my mother was an incredible notetaker and collector. She documented my sports events, stashed away pictures and schoolwork, and even saved a newspaper from the year I was born. When I was old enough to begin selecting items, I was allowed to choose anything meaningful from the year and save it in my special box. I latched onto the idea and wanted to ensure that my entire life was well-documented, that nothing was forgotten. I may have taken it to the extreme, as I was given three long under-the-bed storage bins of special box items when I got married. I imagine my mother was skeptical about many of my chosen items, but she graciously kept her opinions to herself.

You would have expected that I would immediately go through these bins in search of distant memories. Nope. They were my cherished childhood items, and they went under my bed and saw three home moves before I opened them again at the beginning of our minimalist journey. How could I justify keeping the bins with me for years? I reasoned that my childhood would be forgotten without the items; my kids wouldn't know anything about their mother and would be deeply troubled. Ha! When I finally lifted the lid, I reasoned that my kids were more likely to be mortified by the "trash" under the bed and never form any attachment to my keepsakes.

What did I find in my bins, you ask? All of my track times (interesting; I have kept my fastest ones as proof), my Bear Bear (also kept), school photos from every year (kept!), my old orthodontic retainers (gross!), all of my soccer league trophies, every ribbon and award from Bible Drill and flute competitions (I kept one of each, as proof to my children of my many accomplishments!), the creepiest clay mask I ever made in art class, my graduation robe (will I need to graduate high school again?), all the drawings from my second grade sketch book (I'm no Picasso, so goodbye), letters from an elementary pen pal, all my soccer game scores, all my team jerseys, unfinished friendship bracelets, all report cards, and so much more.

While some of these items were interesting and save-worthy, some were downright embarrassing and hilarious. I asked myself, "After I'm gone, will my kids go through these items and treasure them?" The answer was probably no for most of them. My kids will cherish the items that we *use* and make memories with as a family.

I condensed my three bins down to one long bin. We moved twice more before I decided to tackle the bin again in the name of simplifying my life. Some items no longer held any value for me, so it was easy to get rid of them. Remember how I mentioned that your minimalism muscles will grow stronger over time, more aligned with the life that you are developing? I'm pleased to say that the long bin was trashed, and I transferred the remaining items to a small bin that fit in my lap. Much more manageable. I also decided to allow my boys one plastic file box each for their special mementos. They have to curate, only selecting their most important items, and will have one small bin to take with them when they leave home.

"My kids will cherish the items that we **use** and make memories with as a family."

Remember my Bear Bear stuffed animal? I let my boys enjoy him until they were done with him. What purpose did it serve to carry a stuffed bear in a box, never being used? My kids would not hold on to it after I was gone. Surprisingly, my boys loved playing with the bear. Not only was he no longer taking up space in the closet but he was living a renewed second life in my family, even if only for a short time. And I have the memories and a couple pictures of my boys interacting with my Bear Bear from childhood. This is more meaningful to me than storing him in a box.

I realize that many sentimental items are not quirky childhood keepsakes. We also had many heirlooms from grandparents and great-grandparents. Some of these were stored in closets or the garage and never used. Again, what is the purpose of an item except to be used, create memories, and bring joy? We gathered up all the family heirlooms and evaluated what we loved and what we would never use. We kept a couple of our favorite items from each of our forebears and gave the rest away to family or a local thrift store. For example, we were gifted with two sets of china from my husband's grandmother: an elegant, white dinnerware set and a Christmas set. Originally, I was ecstatic, because I had grown up using Christmas dinnerware in my parents' house. Over time, though, I realized that I did not love the Christmas pattern as much as the white china and felt guilty about not using it. I preferred the white china for every occasion, even Christmas. So we parted with the Christmas china and reclaimed the space in a whole kitchen cabinet. We use and enjoy the elegant china regularly. There are extra wins: we save space, we don't feel guilty staring at unused china, and we make fun memories with the boys.

**PRACTICE 14**

# PUT YOUR ITEMS TO WORK

FROM A YOUNG age, I conserved. I am not sure whether I was explicitly taught to conserve or whether it was a result of my personality. I was afraid of running out of things or breaking them. So much so, that I would not even fully use things. Take my American Girl doll stationery, for example. I loved everything American Girl. I owned a doll, clothes, accessories, books, and stationery. While I played with my doll and used most of the accessories, I was stingy with the stationery and stickers. Only my favorite friends ever received a letter from me on American Girl paper, because I didn't want to use it up.

I found a half box of this precious stationery in the bin of kid toys my parents had passed on to me. I dropped it off at the thrift store, hoping that another little girl would find joy from it. How sad that I never fully used it when I had the chance.

After this incident, I deepened my resolve to use what we have to make memories and enhance our lives. Stuff is still stuff at the end of the day, but is it working for me or just hanging around? As I mentioned in the previous chapter, I kept only one set of heirloom china. I also determined to intentionally use the saved china regularly instead of just on special occasions. I moved the set to our normal kitchen cabinet where I could easily reach the plates. We decided to use the china for our weekly Friday sabbath meal. My boys *love* using the china and lighting the candles in their antique holders. Think of how much more meaningful this is for our family than just using the china once a year.

Other examples of this practice include my father-in-law's childhood rocking chair, a T-shirt quilt made by my grandmother, and a toy police car my grandfather owned. Initially, we stored the items with the intent of preserving them. But in light of the Put Your Items to Work practice, we decided to use them, even if they became scratched up or broken over time.

> "I deepened my resolve to use what we have to make memories and enhance our lives. Stuff is still stuff at the end of the day, but is it working for me or just hanging around?"

We put the rocking chair on the porch, and my boys rock in it several times a week. Yes, it is exposed to the elements and requires a staining or coat of protectant every so often, but I would much rather do this than preserve an unused rocking chair. Furthermore, our boys have wonderful memories and pictures of using G-Daddy's rocking chair rather than finding it stored away in the garage decades from now.

I also use my grandmother's T-shirt quilt with the boys. We spread it out on the carpet and lie on it for homeschool and reading. It may eventually get stained, but we are making great memories *using* the quilt. My boys love asking questions about all of the T-shirts preserved in the quilt.

Similarly, our boys play with the police car almost daily. It has gone through wear and tear, but we have memories and joy from playing with it. We love putting items to work in our lives, even if for only a time, rather than endeavoring to preserve them for posterity.

My minimalist journey has helped me become less attached to things and instead allows me to thoroughly enjoy items for the time they are in my life. Things are meant to be used, to support us in reaching our goals, and to enhance the quality of our lives.

## PRACTICE 15

# SEASONAL SLIM-DOWN

ONE OF THE most common ways we acquire stuff is by buying for every season, sport, and holiday. Truly think about it. If I bought decorative items for every major holiday and season where I live, I would own at least thirteen sets of decorations. Don't believe me? Check it out. New Year's, Valentine's Day, St. Patrick's Day, Mardi Gras, Easter, spring, Memorial Day, Fourth of July, fall, football season (aka Roll Tide Roll!), Halloween, Thanksgiving, and Christmas. What! While I have never decorated for all these holidays, I owned enough decorations for a minimum of seven of them. When the items weren't displayed for all to see, they were crammed into storage bins and closets for the other ten to eleven months. I considered this normal; besides, I didn't own a storage unit for my seasonal stuff, so I thought I was doing great!

Nope. I had more than I needed or even wanted. I was completely overwhelmed at the thought of changing out the seasons, and we were drowning in decor. Not only did it take up valuable space for most of the year, but it also took time, energy, and mental reminders to continually rotate through the decorations. Can anyone relate?

Now, I'm not saying that you shouldn't own any seasonal or sports items. I *am* saying that this is a great opportunity to pare down a lot of items and find fulfillment from the time, energy, and space that you regain. Think about how you feel when you put away these items after every holiday. Do you feel joy or the weight of having to change things? Which seasons are most important to you? Which holidays do you want to visually celebrate in your home? Minimize the rotation and choose your most exciting items. You can celebrate most holidays without ever changing the decor.

Once I had reflected on the emotions and feelings I associated with rotating seasonal decor, it was time to eliminate items. Having wreaths for every season and holiday didn't bring me joy. I like having one year-round wreath on the front door that I change out for Christmas, my favorite holiday. I said farewell to my Valentine's and Thanksgiving dishes. I would much rather use my elegant, white china dishes year-round.

I also gave up buying seasonal decorative kitchen towels. Instead, I actually use our decorative towels as kitchen towels—gasp! They are pretty, but I never liked "guarding" the decorative towels in the kitchen; I felt like I was constantly reprimanding my boys or husband to leave the towel alone. This was not the atmosphere I wanted in our home, and the decorative towels just represented more kitchen clutter. After all, towels are a means of cleaning up mess and drying dishes, even if they are pretty.

I chose two seasons to decorate: fall and Christmas. For fall, I use a few handfuls of fake flowers and a wooden "thankful" sign. Fall is my favorite season, so I decorate at the beginning of October. I then whip out the Christmas decorations in early November (yes, before Thanksgiving) to fully enjoy their beauty for two months.

Although I love Christmas, I still minimized my decor for this holiday. Instead of two big trees, I chose my favorite ornaments to adorn one Christmas tree. I stopped hanging onto items that I might someday use; if I did not decorate with it one year, I got rid of it.

The local thrift store was thrilled when we rolled up with armfuls of Christmas items in November. I no longer purchase an ornament for each year. I love the memories and pictures from the year, but I don't always need a physical item to commemorate it. We used to have nativity sets in every room, but we pared them down to our favorites and let the others go. Having fewer Christmas items means it takes less time and energy to set up and take down every year. I also more fully enjoy the items I kept.

Ask yourself: Which holidays do you enjoy representing in your home? Which seasons bring you pleasure in the process of decorating? Do you sense any hesitation or frustration about rotating this stuff? If so, fully engage with your feelings and figure out why. Commit to getting rid of anything you are not using through the minimalism process I laid out earlier, and celebrate how freeing it is to own less, store less, and rotate fewer items. Slimming down on holiday items frees you up to more fully enjoy the holiday.

## PRACTICE 16

# MINDFUL TOY MANAGEMENT

**ONE OF MY** biggest minimalist revelations occurred in managing my kids' toys. A popular idea in American culture is to rotate toys for entertainment and sanity purposes. Toys and games are stored in bins and rotated in and out of the playing space after a set time. The reasoning is that toys get played with and kids don't get bored.

I have concluded that this is one of the most ridiculous ideas that I embraced. Let's be real. Storing toys in closets for months on end not only depended on me *remembering* that they were there but also required my *time* to switch out the toys for the sake of my kids' entertainment.

As I have grown as a parent, educator, and person, I've realized that *entertaining* my children is not one of my life's goals. My focus is on inspiring creativity, generosity, simplicity, joy, and excellence in their lives. I don't think keeping my kids constantly entertained is a healthy practice—for me or them. There is value in modeling slowing down throughout the week and being content with what we have. I purposely aim to decrease the volume of stimuli that my kids experience, allowing their minds to grow and develop through problem-solving and creativity. A room—and closets—packed full of toys does not set my kids up to be content and enjoy what they own.

Instead, we minimized the toys, keeping what they played with and enjoyed. I included the boys in the process, setting up our family "why" for minimalism and asking them to identify their favorite toys. We provided certain boundaries, specified a quantity of items they could keep, and empowered them to choose with intention what they wanted to own.

I then designated a bookcase in their room for toy bins. I grouped toys into similar categories: sports balls, music and puzzles, animals and cars, books, blocks, and Legos. They live on the bookcase, with a few exceptions that are in the closet: the long race car track, the art bin (so they can't access coloring items without me), and stuffed animals. Everything in the bookshelf is visible in organized and labeled bins, so the boys can easily decide what to play with. They only remove one bin at a time—or two if they are being extra creative (e.g., making a Lego zoo for their animals). This makes for easy cleanup, because all the toys go into that one bin. Honestly, my boys mainly take care of the clean-up process themselves.

> "I purposely aim to decrease the volume of stimuli that my kids experience, allowing their minds to grow and develop through problem-solving and creativity."

This setup is amazing for several reasons. First, we are living our best minimalist life and using what we own. Second, we can easily see which bin the boys have chosen, so we occasionally minimize more toys when we notice that some are no longer being played with. Third, cleanup is so much easier, because the toys are organized in bins and my boys can tidy them away independently. Fourth, toys are no longer abandoned in a closet, and fifth, I no longer have to remember to rotate toys.

The result: my kids own toys that they love and use. When that is no longer the case, we are thankful for the time with the toy and then release it to someone else who will use it. We keep the toys minimized by implementing the Mindful Exchange. If our boys get new animals, books, or toys for their birthdays, they (or we) decide which items will be replaced based on what is unused or worn out. We celebrate the fact that toys, books, and animals are well-used; it means creativity is growing and memories are being made. Toy management has never been easier or more rewarding.

## PRACTICE 17

# PURPOSEFUL PURSUITS

**AFTER A FEW** years of minimalism, it was time to tackle my shelf of hobbies. I had not attempted to analyze my hobbies before that, because I knew it would be hard. I am sentimental about some of them and have a fear of missing out.

My work with minimalism so far had taught me that in order to find my ideal level of freedom I had to deal with my beliefs and perspectives before dealing with the stuff. I began with a deep-dive reflection and journaling. I started by taking inventory of how I currently spent my free, or fun, time. What were my purposeful pursuits in this season of life? This was an *essential* question. Just because I'd been a scrapbooker and an avid track runner in my teens didn't mean that I had to continue these pursuits now.

As I listed my current hobbies, I paid attention to the emotions that emerged. I felt *guilty* for not continuing certain hobbies. In a weird way, I felt that I had somehow wasted time building skills when I was younger if I was no longer going to pursue those hobbies. I continued journaling diligently, working through my emotions and posture toward my hobbies.

I emerged on the other side with some clarity. I recalled great memories with friends and family, as well as by myself. Those hobbies had helped me build valuable life skills—precision, dedication, endurance, creativity, and habit-building. They were not a waste of time. On the contrary, they were a valuable part of my life that had molded me into who I am today.

I also remembered that my time on this earth is finite. Did I want to spend my time doing things that I wasn't passionate or excited about? I remembered to extend grace to myself—none of this was a waste of time, nor had I failed as a person. Rather, these hobbies and purposeful pursuits had been in my life for a season, and I had enjoyed them. It was time to practice gratitude and let go of some of them. It was okay for some hobbies to be limited to a certain period of my life.

I determined that my purposeful pursuits should be creative, inspirational, and enjoyable activities that allowed me to recharge or extend my impact in the world.

Having done the heart and mind work, I reflected on how I would like to spend my time if I had a free Saturday afternoon. Hiking, walking with the family, playing board games, writing, reading novels, practicing languages on Duolingo, and working out were some of the main activities I brainstormed. I committed to go through my shelf and see which hobbies lined up with my current ideas of fun. A few of my previous hobbies had survived several moves without being used. I didn't want to feel guilty about my past hobbies anymore. Instead, I determined that my purposeful pursuits should be creative, inspirational, and enjoyable activities that allowed me to recharge or extend my impact in the world.

I was now ready to address the physical space and hobby items. Picking up one item at a time, I asked, "Does this hobby still bring me great joy or help me attain my personal, relational, and professional goals?" Due to my perspective pivot, I was willing to say goodbye to some hobbies, expressing gratitude for past opportunities.

What did I actually release? I had been a scrapbooker for many years but hadn't scrapbooked for a decade. My left-handed golf clubs, soccer cleats, and track cleats were all from high school. Though I loved those sports and had fond memories, I hadn't used the equipment since I graduated. I figured that I could always rent golf clubs or buy new cleats if I ever joined an adult track team for slow runners!

I'd had phases of learning how to cross-stitch, write calligraphy, draw, play basic piano, and freezer cook, each with its own materials. In addition, I had my old bike from growing up, voice lesson sheet music from middle school (in case I ever needed to sing "My Heart Will Go On"), stacks of cool puzzles that had either been partially assembled or never even started, and my old sewing kit. Seriously, no one person can possibly have time to pursue all these hobbies.

When I asked myself how I desired to spend my time in this season, none of my old hobbies made it onto the list. I knew that to make room for the wonderful pursuits in my present life stage, I needed to relinquish items taking up physical, emotional, and mental residence every time I saw them. Life is too short to live with regrets and guilt. I practiced gratitude and felt immense relief when I released my old hobbies. I no longer felt that I was missing out; instead, I was delighted that I was intentionally choosing my current life pursuits. How freeing and grace-filled it is to know that I choose how I spend my time.

## PRACTICE 18

# SPARK THE START ONE ITEM AT A TIME

•○—•◯•—○•

**ONE OF MY** favorite life tips for habit formation came from a life-changing book, *Atomic Habits.* The premise is that one way to begin a new habit or lifestyle change is to make it so incredibly easy that you cannot help but do it. James Clear references a story about a guy who flossed one tooth a day for a certain amount of time, even if he wanted to do more. The idea is that the action took minimal effort and helped him do the most difficult part: creating a habit in the context of an already structured day. Eventually, he added a tooth, and before long, he was flossing all his teeth daily. I have used this practice to begin many habits in my life, including minimalism.[14]

I reached a point in my minimalism journey when the systematic Zone-Focused Resets in our home stopped. I was super pregnant with my second child, chasing a toddler around, working full-time, and preparing to buy a house and move across the neighborhood. I knew I only had a couple months to minimize more of our stuff before baby number two arrived; I was majorly feeling the nesting urgency! But I was tired and stuck, so I decided to implement Clear's habit starter by committing to minimize one item a day.

I was still systematically going through my house, but for the first week, I permitted myself to give or trash only one item per day. This was so ridiculously easy that I couldn't excuse myself from the process. The second week, I accomplished up to five minutes of minimizing a space if I felt like it. I was working toward momentum and sustainability, and the results were incredible.

By the end of the first month, I was minimizing five minutes a day most days of the week. It may not sound like a lot, but that is enough to go through a whole shelf, and the progress gained momentum. Starting on such a small scale helped me reach my larger goals. This is a fantastic practice to spark momentum and motivation during a busy or stuck time of life.

## PRACTICE 19

# ONE-ITEM RESET

DO YOU REMEMBER my drop zone story in the Explosion chapter? I wish I could say that was the only time this ever happened, but an extremely busy or weird scheduling week tends to temporarily break the system. Our drop zone once again became a muddled mess, presenting an opportunity to acknowledge my humanity and analyze my routines.

My husband was out of town for almost a week, and I was heavily pregnant with our third boy. It was the final week of school before Christmas break, packed with festivities that called for my involvement as both a teacher and a mom. Some evenings it was all I could do to brush my teeth and climb into bed right after putting the boys down. Consequently, our drop zone became increasingly chaotic day by day. Feeling exhausted, I gave myself grace, knowing that I could tackle the pile at the end of the week.

The end of the week came and went. My exhaustion and anxiety about the pile grew every time I walked past the drop zone to throw in a load of laundry, let the dog out, or grab my purse. This situation revealed that I sometimes needed to find encouragement and motivation in a different practice, even after years of minimizing.

Enter a slightly modified practice of Practice 18: the One-Item Reset. For the next couple of days, I purposed that every time I walked past the drop zone (about a dozen times a day), I had to transfer just *one* item to its proper home. After a few trips of moving candy and junk mail to the trash and taping up a ripped book and returning it to my boys' room, I began to see progress and the bottom of the counter again!

I continued like this the next few days until the drop zone was completely back to its desired state. It didn't become picture-perfect instantly, but this practice provided immediate motivation as I saw small yet attainable progress. It kept the momentum going until the area was conquered and ready to be guarded again.

While my ultimate desire is to minimize an area and then guard it from clutter, sometimes life happens. This practice provided a scaffolded approach that fit my circumstances and schedule at that time. The One-Item Reset works great for surface areas (kitchen counter, living room floor) or other spaces you encounter often. It relates to the Daily Reset habits that form the daily habits of your life and is a productive temporary approach to resetting a zone with minimal effort.

## PRACTICE 20

# HARMONIOUS LIVING WITH OTHERS

**DO YOU EVER** wonder if this minimalist lifestyle is just for single professionals? I can attest that while a single human can (not always) own fewer items than a five-person household, minimalism is for any size family. With that in mind, though, you may have realized that living with others can be as challenging and frustrating as it is fun and rewarding. Living in harmony with others requires recognition and acceptance of their personalities, quirks, dreams, and, yes, stuff. While our family practices minimalism together, it doesn't look the same for each individual.

> Living in harmony with others requires recognition and acceptance of their personalities, quirks, dreams, and, yes, stuff.

My husband and I started the minimalism journey together. We have walked through the process in many areas together, but I have gone through our home's areas more frequently than he has. I have discovered that I *love* the systematic minimizing process. Aaron sporadically minimizes when he notices a need. We have created a flow in which I periodically reset areas of our home, dealing with necessary items and setting aside any items that require his consultation. Does this mean that Aaron doesn't minimize? Absolutely not. He is great about immediately dealing with items as they enter our home, only buying what we use and need, employing the Mindful Exchange, guarding areas, and getting rid of items or toys that no longer belong. My approach may be more systematic, but his approach depends on when the situations arise. Both are helpful for continuing our minimalist journey and carving out the life we desire. We are both equally committed to intentional owning, because we have witnessed the great benefits of minimalism.

There are areas that I do not minimize. These spaces include Aaron's clothes drawers, his nightstand, his work bag, his hats, and his stack of books. While these spaces may include different or more items than I would choose, I respect him and his journey to manage his possessions. We have an understanding that we will communicate if another person's clutter begins to infringe on common space or become a stressor. That doesn't mean things will change, just that a conversation occurs, reminding ourselves of our shared vision and perspective.

Similarly, I give my boys some autonomy in their spaces. My oldest has five art pieces hanging on his wall. He can choose whatever pictures he wants to place there (even if I don't understand his choice). Whenever he brings home new artwork, he has a choice to make: give the artwork to someone to brighten their day, swap it out with a piece on the wall, or throw it away. It is amazing to watch a five-year-old analyze his artwork. Small humans are also capable of making intentional decisions and curating their collections.

Another area where our two oldest boys have autonomy is with their rock collections. They each have a box where they can collect as many amazing fossils, shells, rocks, and, sometimes, snails as they want. But the items must remain in the box. In both examples—artwork and rocks—my boys have freedom and choice within preset boundaries that allow them to experience life while not living in complete cluttered chaos.

Minimalism does not encourage control over other people. It should not incorporate dominance or self-righteousness. Living with others requires compromise and grace. Minimalism is a journey that each person experiences in their own way. I can compromise and set boundaries, but ultimately, there may be more tools and hats in the house than I would like. And that is okay, because I have learned to communicate, encourage, compromise, and let go. When all is said and done, I want these humans in my life and my home more than I want one solitary hammer or one shelf of hats.

Remember to cherish relationships more than stuff. This will bring harmony to living and minimizing with others.

“Living with others requires compromise and grace. Minimalism is a journey that each person experiences in their own way.”

## CHAPTER 7

# REFLECTION ON CONSCIOUS LIVING

**DO YOU EVER** feel overwhelmed by the suffering and darkness in our world? Do you ever seek to see the light and positivity but struggle to do so? Many times, even with faith, support, and a positive attitude, I still grieve the hardship in my own life and the lives of others. Believe it or not, real suffering happens in *everyone's* life outside of social media. We just don't talk about it all the time, and this can cause us to feel lonely and lost.

Prayer, journaling, meditating, crying, and talking with my husband or a friend help me process my thoughts and feelings. But I am thankful for the hard moments, because they help me empathize and connect with others, my God, and myself. They also prompt me to remember the important things in life beyond my job, my family, my perspective, and social media. They enable me to deeply feel the grief in this world, which makes the joys all the sweeter.

You might be wondering how in the world this relates to minimalism. Joshua Becker defines minimalism as "the intentional promotion of the things that bring you joy and the removal of those that do not."[15] You might be thinking, "Lauren, I don't feel *any* joy right now, just frustration, anger, and grief!" That is a valid point.

I have found that because I have minimized and am continuing to find ways to minimize, elevating some things in my life and removing others, I have more space to process my emotions. I have fewer daily house tasks and less clutter hanging over my head while I am deep in my emotions. Space to process is such a healthy gift to give myself. I am free to connect more deeply with myself and my God, and I sometimes experience growth and breakthroughs. Isn't personal development one of our main goals in life?

Furthermore, practicing minimalism has freed up my resources, finances, and time so that I can engage with some of the problems in our world. I have learned to grapple with my feelings and be attentive to the suffering—in mine and others' lives—that is breaking my heart. I am then able to ponder how I can give of myself and my resources to respond to these issues. I would far rather help someone else than buy another pair of shoes or a new purse. Minimalism allows me a greater opportunity to partner with those who advocate for causes I am passionate about and change others' lives. Wouldn't that be more rewarding and meaningful than 90 percent of what we spend our money on? How can we find ways to enrich, empower, and bring freedom to other people's lives?

I feel the shift in myself as I am writing, reflecting on purchases I was considering for later in the week. But how can any physical item take a higher priority than people? Most of this perspective goes back to finding the space and quiet to process your journey, emotions, and trials to enable you to grow and bear fruit that changes people's lives. What a great gift we have in minimalism—to provide this space and free up resources.

I include the thoughts in this chapter to remind us both that life is about more than stuff and the purging of stuff. Life is about people, your impact, your faith, your family, and your God-given potential. I can't wait to see how minimalism helps you cut the clutter and create a life that matters.

## CHAPTER 8

# NOW WHAT?

**SO WHERE DOES** this leave us? I have shared my journey and valuable practices I learned along the way. Now that you have this knowledge, what are you going to do with it? Has your perspective pivoted as you've read this book? My hope is that you view your resources in a fresh light and feel encouraged to minimize your possessions and lighten other weights in your life—all in pursuit of a purposeful, intentional, and joyful life.

Only *you* have particular talents, resources, and experiences to offer the world. Someone out there needs you to rise to the occasion so their life can be changed for the better. We are all connected. When one person rises to their potential for the good of humanity, others are changed and given similar resources or opportunities to reach for their God-given potential and purpose. The connection causes ripple effects—others need you!

So what are your next steps? Continue walking through the process of minimalism to achieve the threshold of resources that maximize your living. Join communities of minimalists, or at least find a friend to whom you are accountable. Return to this book often for inspiration and motivation. Buy this book for a friend to inspire their journey. Document your minimalist journey with photos and share your story with others on social media. Follow me on social media for inspiration and answers to your minimalist questions. Visit my website, www.ownwithintention.com, to find community, coaching, podcasts, and more.

Who you are makes a difference! Others need you to rise to the occasion. Start discovering how you can own with intention and change the world.

# ACKNOWLEDGMENTS

**THANKFUL TO THE** Lord for my life experience, this message, and the opportunity to share it. I'm beyond grateful to help others create change and step into their God-given potential.

Thank you to Aaron. My husband, my best friend and greatest encourager. Your belief and support help me continue leaning forward in faith, trusting that I was called and equipped to write this book.

Thank you to my boys. Your love, laughter, and joy for life remind me daily of my why.

Thank you to Kathryn Gordon for believing in me and this manuscript from the beginning. You are a big reason why this message is making its way into the world!

Thank you to all of my original readers: Mom, Dad, Carl, Ginger, Wendy, Selah, Kathryn, and Aaron. Your insight is invaluable, and your belief in this message helps me trust that it needs to reach many more people!

Thank you to my publishing team for bringing every detail of this book to life. I am deeply grateful for your professionalism, guidance, and care.

Thank you, reader!! Thank you for trusting me with your time and attention. My hope is that these pages point you to what matters most and that you find inspiration, freedom, and transformation as you begin your minimalist journey. You are worth it, and you have so much to contribute to the world!

# ENDNOTES

1. Marie Kondo, *The Life-Changing Magic of Tidying Up: The Japanese Art of Decluttering and Organizing* (Ten Speed Press, 2014).

2. B. J. Fogg, *Tiny Habits: The Small Changes That Change Everything* (Houghton Mifflin Harcourt, 2020).

3. James Clear, *Atomic Habits: An Easy & Proven Way to Build Good Habits & Break Bad Ones* (Avery Publishing, 2018).

4. Charles Duhigg, *The Power of Habit: Why We Do What We Do in Life and Business* (Random House Trade Paperbacks, 2012).

5. Joshua Becker, *The More of Less: Finding the Life You Want Under Everything You Own* (WaterBrook Press, 2016).

6. Joshua Becker, *The Minimalist Home: A Room-by-Room Guide to a Decluttered, Focused Life* (WaterBrook Press, 2019).

7. Clear, *Atomic Habits*, 84.

8. Clear, *Atomic Habits*, 27.

9. "Consistency Compounds!" John Maxwell, YouTube, accessed July 3, 2025, https://www.youtube.com/watch?v=M6-2E32w3nE.

10. Oprah Winfrey, "Quotes," Goodreads, accessed July 1, 2025, https://www.goodreads.com/quotes/2646-the-more-you-praise-and-celebrate-your-life-the-more.

11. Fogg, *Tiny Habits*, 155.

12. Becker, *The More of Less*, 173 (chapter 11).

13. Fogg, *Tiny Habits*, 11.

14. Clear, *Atomic Habits*, 143.

15. Becker, *The More of Less*, 136.

Thank you for investing in this book.

I would love to stay connected with you beyond these pages. Scan the QR code below to connect with me and access additional resources!

Book Resources

www.ingramcontent.com/pod-product-compliance
Lightning Source LLC
LaVergne TN
LVHW090530110826
845146LV00003B/1043

* 9 7 9 8 9 0 3 7 2 0 0 5 7 *